I SHALL NOT DIE
My Walk Through the Valley of Death

Cathy Dillard Byrum

WESTBOW
PRESS®
A DIVISION OF THOMAS NELSON
& ZONDERVAN

WestBow Press books may be ordered through booksellers or by contacting:

WestBow Press
A Division of Thomas Nelson & Zondervan
1663 Liberty Drive
Bloomington, IN 47403
www.westbowpress.com
1 (866) 928-1240

ISBN: 978-1-9736-6031-6 (sc)
ISBN: 978-1-9736-6032-3 (hc)
ISBN: 978-1-9736-6033-0 (e)

Library of Congress Control Number: 2019904520

Print information available on the last page.

WestBow Press rev. date: 5/24/2019

This book is dedicated to Jesus, my Savior, Lord, and healer, and to my mom, who always seemed to know I would one day write a book.

PREFACE

If you were to describe me, one thing you could say is I am slow but thorough. That has definitely been the case with this book. I began writing at the prompting of my husband, Ronnie, who put a legal pad in my lap and pen in my hand as we were on the road to a family reunion at the end of July 2015 (he was driving!).

In addition to its inception on the highway during that trip, parts of the book have since come into being in many places: on the road to Omaha for my one-year checkup after the transplant; in a covered outdoor café on a rainy afternoon in Antigua, Guatemala, watching my grandson sleep in his stroller; in a coffee shop in Cave Springs, Arkansas, on a rainy Saturday morning; during many late nights at home, because I am still working full time; and most recently on a hotel balcony during a short trip to Orlando.

I have written in bits and pieces, with rather long breaks in between, because I have found it to be both cathartic and emotionally draining to re-live the whole experience. There is an upside, however, in that every time I came back to it, I was once again humbled, being reminded that but for the grace of God manifested through a modern-day miracle, I would not be here. Yes, I had top-notch medical care, but even my doctor told me after it all, "You shouldn't be here!"

Twice, in June and November 2014, I thought the whole cancer thing was done and I could get back to "normal." I have realized since that it will never be done. Being a cancer survivor will forever be part of who I am now. I am reminded of that every time someone says "I have a friend who has cancer, can you share your story?"

I have been asked at what point I knew I would survive. It was soon after the start of it all, when I read Psalm 118:17, "I shall not die, but live, and declare the works of the Lord." Thus, the title of this book.

I never made a deal with God, but the verse has two parts. God came through on the first part; now it's my turn.

CHAPTER 1
Never Get Sick

I have always been a healthy person. The only times I recall even using my health insurance were when my two sons were born in 1989 and 1990, and when I broke my leg in 2000. That's how I explain the fact that I gave little notice to two jelly bean–sized bumps at the base of my neck, near my left collar bone, when they first appeared around December 2013.

The following month, January 2014, was a busy one. My youngest son, Dan, had taken a job in another city, and so I did what I could to help him get moved and settled. At the same time, his older brother, Derick, had completed two years of missionary work in Nepal and was preparing to return to the United States. He had long wanted to visit the Holy Land, and so had I. Knowing I would likely see very little of him once he returned home because he had a serious girlfriend, I decided to meet him in London, and we flew together from there to Israel. While there, we walked up and down the hills of Jerusalem, took an all-day bus tour, and hauled his two years' worth of stuff through hotels and airports.

I mention all of this to show I had no pain or lack of energy, which are common symptoms of the silent killer that I carried, unbeknownst to me. I did lose some weight, which by the time I noticed it, I attributed to the above activities and accompanying stress.

The bumps on my neck weren't painful and didn't get bigger, but they didn't get smaller or go away either. When I finally mentioned them to my husband, Ronnie, he urged me to make a doctor's appointment to have them checked. On March 13, 2014, a Thursday, I went to a doctor I found on a Find a Physician website. I didn't even have a primary care doctor—I had never needed one!

I saw Kelly, the physician assistant, that day. After examining the bumps, he ordered an X-ray, mentioning the possibility of there being additional lumps in my armpits. While waiting on the X-ray in a gown, I reached way up into my left armpit, where I found what felt like a bag of marbles. After the X-ray, Kelly told me he was going to schedule a mammogram and ultrasound for early the next week.

Two days later, Saturday March 15, Ronnie and I went to Springfield, Missouri, about a two-hour drive from our home in Rogers, Arkansas, for a cow sale we attended every year. Later that day, I got a call that my mom was ill, and so we drove the two hours back home, stopping only long enough to pack a bag. We headed to Oklahoma City to see her, making the three-and-a-half-hour drive in the opposite direction. We stayed in Oklahoma City through Sunday. While there, I didn't tell any of my family about my own appointments or what were, by this time, nagging suspicions.

On Monday, March 17, I had the mammogram and ultrasound, which we were told were inconclusive. Kelly said he would schedule a CT scan of my neck and chest next. He had told me he was being extra cautious because he had recently lost a friend to cancer. I had had no symptoms except for the lumps on my neck and in my armpit, and so I was not overly concerned at this point. Besides, with Derick being back home after two years and Dan having moved and started a new job, there was plenty to distract me.

The level of distraction escalated in a wonderful way when Derick proposed to his girlfriend, Jill, on Saturday, March 29!

The CT scan was the following Friday, April 4. It came with a referral to yet another doctor, this time an ear, nose, and throat specialist. That seemed odd to me, but he explained that ENTs deal with anything from the neck up.

The appointment was scheduled for Monday, April 7. I went to see him right after work, and he performed a needle biopsy right then and there in his office. He told me he would call with results rather than have me come back in to find out, if that was okay with me.

After having had an X-ray, mammogram, ultrasound, CT scan, and now a needle biopsy over a period of three and a half weeks, it was more than okay with me. I was ready to know what was up! I was ready to be done with all this medical stuff—or so I thought.

I did my best to stay busy while I waited for the call, which finally came three days later, on Thursday, April 10. The ENT doctor called personally. I didn't have time to wonder why because he wasted no time before telling me the diagnosis was non-Hodgkin's lymphoma.

It may have been his experience that led him to not use the word *cancer*, but for me that was a gift. I didn't even realize it was cancer at first until I looked it up. I don't deal with surprises well at all, and the fact that he avoided that word allowed me time to slowly slip into my new identity as a cancer patient.

The first planning meeting for Derick and Jill's wedding

was that same evening, only hours after I had learned of my diagnosis. I already had my dress for the wedding and planned to take it to show the bride and her mother. I was not going to miss this first meeting, and so I didn't tell anyone my news till after, and then only my husband. He was the only one who knew of the tests I'd been having anyway.

After the bride's mom and I tried on our dresses, we sat around the table with Derick, Jill, a couple of her sisters, and the wedding planner and discussed plans for the wedding and reception. That was when I first learned to live in the moment. I had no idea what even the near future held, and not knowing how many of the wedding festivities I would get to enjoy, I made a point to enjoy that evening thoroughly.

$\mathcal{N}$ow What?

CHAPTER 2

On Monday, April 14, after having four days to adjust to the news, Ronnie and I went to a follow-up appointment with the ENT doctor. We were anxious to move forward as quickly as possible with treatment and asked if the next step was for him to refer us to an oncologist. We will never forget his response. "It won't do any good. Your spleen and liver look like swiss cheese." I asked for copies of the test results. This was when I learned to be selective about to whom I chose to listen!

The next day on the way to work, I called my friend Aimee and, without telling her why, asked if she could have lunch with me that day. She was an oncology nurse, and I knew Tuesday was her day off. As soon as she walked into the sandwich shop where we were meeting, I showed her the reports. She called a fellow nurse at Highlands Oncology Group (affectionately referred to as HOG) and asked if there was any possible way for me to see Dr. Pat Travis right away. Dr. Travis is one of the best lymphoma specialists in the country who just happens to be in practice in the same city where I live. Another friend, Joe, a retired pharmaceutical salesman, had also recommended Dr. Travis. It was Dr. Travis's nurse, Anne, whom Aimee had called, and they arranged for me to be seen right away.

Two days later, April 17, I had my first appointment with Dr. Travis. He said from what he had seen, I had one of the more aggressive types of non-Hodgkin's lymphoma. Although they hadn't completely narrowed down yet which type, he would treat it aggressively. He initially said treatment would be six rounds of chemo, one every three weeks.

I asked if I would be able to continue working, and he replied he didn't see why not. I told him I absolutely had to be at my son's wedding on June 21; he saw no problem with that. I was even hoping to make a cruise in July that had been a gift from my boss the previous Christmas. Dr. Travis thought he might be able to work the treatments around that as well.

The ENT doctor had scheduled an outpatient procedure for the following day to remove one of the nodes on my neck. I asked Dr. Travis if it was necessary to go ahead with that procedure, because it was already determined that I had non-Hodgkin's lymphoma. He said there were forty-two types of NHL, and he needed the node to be biopsied to determine which variety I had.

The next day was Good Friday. Surgery to have the node removed was an outpatient procedure and was done early that morning. Ronnie and I had lunch afterward with our pastor and his wife, who was one of my closest friends. Pastor Scott asked me if I was going to tell the church on Sunday about my illness. I said, "Do you really think Easter Sunday is the time to do that?" referring to the fact that there would be a lot of visitors attending.

He replied, "What better time?" I told him it depended on if I could get both my sons together to tell them first. I wanted to tell them in person and together, and with their schedules, that was not easy to accomplish!

The following day, Saturday, I planned a dinner with

6

Derick and Dan so that I could tell them before announcing to the church the next morning. I used the excuse that Easter Sunday was hectic, and we could have a more relaxed dinner by doing it on Saturday evening. They both agreed, but as it turned out, they each had something come up and couldn't make it for dinner.

I had also invited my friend Donna to dinner the same evening. Donna is a friend from church and is a widow whose husband had died of cancer. We had also just lost our friend Betty to cancer ten months before. I promised Donna this would not end the same way. I am a realist and am not prone to making empty promises. When those words came out of my mouth, it surprised me as much as it did her. I really had nothing on which to base such a promise. The situation was certainly beyond my control.

On Easter Sunday, I finally got both my sons together at home before church and told them the news. It wasn't the ideal situation in terms of timing, but I needed to tell them. I assured them this would end well. Again, I had nothing on which to base this statement other than the sense of peace I felt. Things had happened so quickly that I had not had time to fully consider the possible outcomes.

For a couple of weeks, the pastor had been asking the church to pray for "a member with a serious health problem." Following the Easter service, he called me up to the microphone. I told the church that when I first heard my diagnosis by phone ten days earlier, I did not panic or fall apart. I had peace and knew where I would go when I died.

Then I shared that I had told God there were some people I wanted to see saved first, and that some of them were in the room that day!

CHAPTER 3
Not Ready, Set, Go

The next day, Easter Monday, April 21, began a week of events happening in rapid succession. I had a pre-op appointment in preparation for surgery to insert a chemo port the following day. If you're unfamiliar with what that is, it is a device inserted under the skin through which chemotherapy drugs are administered without a patient having to be stuck with needles repeatedly.

The surgery to insert the port on Tuesday afternoon was again an outpatient procedure. The port that was now inserted into my chest wall was a constant reminder that brought home the reality of what was about to commence.

I'd been told I would lose my hair as a side effect from the chemo drugs, and so I decided to be proactive and purchase a wig on Wednesday. My friend Aimee and future daughter-in-law Jill had both recommended the same shop, Custom Designs. Sara Lou, the owner and stylist, would become a dear friend. She had a wig in stock that was very similar to my own hair. She trimmed a few bangs on it, and I was set.

Later the same day, I also had a CT scan of my abdomen and pelvis.

Friday of that week was April 25 and was the first day of

my actual treatment plan. The schedule for the day included a bone marrow biopsy and a PET scan. It was at this point that the whole strategy and tempo changed. Dr. Travis learned from these two tests that not only was the cancer in my liver, spleen, and all my lymph nodes, but 87 percent of my bone marrow was involved.

It was also on this day that, without directly or even intentionally doing it, Dr. Travis said something that gave me hope. As I lay on my side for the marrow biopsy, he made an observation and simple statement, both of which were filled with life and the future. He said, "Did you know you have some slight scoliosis? It probably won't ever give you any trouble, though, because you're slim."

I don't think I've ever mentioned to him how much that meant to me.

I had been given Demerol for the marrow biopsy, which I had forgotten I did not tolerate well, and so I was very foggy and unable to even stand on my own. As I sat in a wheelchair coming out from under the effects of the drug, Ronnie broke the news to me that instead of six rounds of chemo three weeks apart, I would check into the hospital the following Monday for a solid week of chemo.

Before leaving HOG that Friday afternoon following the marrow biopsy, I received two bags of fluids in the chemo room; the fluid would raise my pH to protect my kidneys from the drugs I would be receiving the following week. This was the first time to use my port. Due to the Demerol effects, I didn't even remember having been in the chemo room for fluids that day.

I checked into the hospital on Monday, April 28, for five days of chemo. Ronnie stayed with me day and night, and our friend Joe came every day to tell us about the drugs I was being given and to make sure I got what I needed to keep me from getting sick. Prior to his retirement, Joe's specialty as a pharmaceutical salesman had been oncology drugs.

Anne, Dr. Travis's nurse, had promised, "You won't throw up your toenails!"

It was an uneventful week, and Anne's promise proved true. I still felt good and was even able to work some via my laptop from my hospital room.

I was amazed at how quickly the lumps (which I now knew to be lymph nodes) on my neck, in my armpits, and at the tops of my legs, disappeared. I remember thinking, "Okay, this is good. They're going away. This is working!" I completed the week of round-the-clock chemo and went home on Friday, May 2, to rest and recover.

CHAPTER 4

$\mathcal{H}$earts and (No) Flowers

On Sunday evening, May 4, our church had a wedding shower for Derick and Jill. I was determined to go, and I ate a lot of Mexican food that evening. I knew the chemo aftereffects would kick in at some point and I would lose my appetite, so I wanted to gain a little ground before that happened!

What I didn't know was that this would be the last of the prewedding festivities I would be able to attend.

During the night, I woke at two in the morning feeling like my heart had exited my chest and was jumping up and down on it. At first, I thought maybe it was because of the Mexican food. After making a call to the Highlands Oncology nurse on call, Ronnie took me to the emergency room at the hospital. There, we learned I was experiencing rapid a-fib, or atrial fibrillation, which is, in simplest terms, a very fast irregular heartbeat. Mine was 171 beats per minute at the time. In the ER, they got it under control with medication.

After having spent the previous week in the hospital, I stayed all day Monday and that night for observation. My cardiologist came in to discuss the two medications I would now be taking. He told me that due to possible side effects from the medication, he would schedule a baseline pulmonary (lung) function test and heart stress test.

The pattern was beginning to become apparent: more tests, more drugs, more tests.

After being released from the hospital on Tuesday, May 6, I went straight to HOG for a previously scheduled Neupogen shot (to stimulate blood cell production) and a lumbar puncture. The puncture was to draw spinal fluid to test for cancer cells and to inject chemo drugs as a precautionary measure. It's not as unpleasant as it might sound. On Thursday of that week, I had an appointment for a routine blood draw (I learned quickly blood is drawn every visit), steroid shot, and chemo session.

In the midst of wedding planning, Jill would come sit with me when she could, to give Ronnie a break. Derick and Dan had both just started new jobs and would come when they could.

After five days of chemo in the hospital the previous week and another trip to the hospital to start this week, the end of the week was blissfully boring. This was largely due to the fact that thanks to the onslaught of the chemo drugs doing what they were intended to do to my body, I had little to no immunity and was on doctor-ordered isolation. I couldn't leave the house, and no one could come in.

This meant I couldn't even go to church, and that Sunday was Mother's Day. Dan, Derick, and Jill went to church, and afterward they came to the house to see me. They had to wear masks just to come inside, but we dropped the masks behind our backs long enough for the traditional Mother's Day picture! They had brought me flowers that had been given to all the moms in the service, but those had to remain outside on the porch because fresh flowers, fruits, and vegetables were prohibited for those with compromised immune systems.

We dropped the masks long enough to capture a Mother's Day picture, despite my being on isolation due to the chemo. This is the last picture before I lost my hair just days later.

CHAPTER 5

The Hairs on Your Head Are Numbered

Everyone knows chemo causes hair to fall out. We've all seen friends, family members, or other women wearing the telltale headscarves. As the most visible evidence of what we go through as cancer/chemo patients, the subject deserves some detail here.

From my first week in the hospital for round-the-clock chemo, Dr. Travis didn't mince words with me. He was accustomed to my questions from the start. I asked if there was a chance I wouldn't lose my hair. His answer: "I'll get your hair!" When I asked when, he told me ten to fourteen days, and he was right.

But no one told me how it would happen or what it would feel like. I didn't know whether it would be gradual, or whether I'd wake up one morning and find it all on my pillow! From talking with my stylist since that time, and from what I've read, it can be a very emotional experience for many women. It was not so much so for me, but still I don't like surprises, and I wanted to be prepared and know what to expect.

Sara Lou is the owner and stylist of Custom Designs, the shop where I got my wig. She has a heart for women with thinning hair, especially cancer patients. From the name of the shop, I had assumed I would have to order a wig, but she had one in stock that was similarly styled and shoulder-length like my hair. It was a little darker in color, but I had been highlighting my hair for so many years that I had been wanting to go a little darker anyway. She recommended a synthetic wig because they hold their style better and are easier to care for, whereas human hair wigs must be styled and treated just as one's own hair would.

I knew the wig would be expensive, but it was not as much as I thought. It was hand tied, which added to the cost but made it much more natural looking. And when I compared the cost of the wig to what I would have spent on my hair during the ten months I wore it, it put the cost in perspective!

Many times over the years, I had considered trying a shorter haircut, but I never had the nerve or the patience to let it grow back out if I didn't like it. If I had this to do over again, knowing I was going to lose my hair, I would get that short haircut before losing the hair. It would have made the shedding process much more manageable. As it happened, I "let my hair go" before it let go, thinking that the worse it looked, the less I'd miss it! I didn't have it trimmed or highlighted, so it looked less than lovely by the time it fell out.

About a week into Dr. Travis's estimated time range of ten to fourteen days, I noticed I was shedding rather heavily. I wondered how long the molting process would take when, on the morning of May 13, I woke up and noticed my hair was heavily matted on the back of my head.

I was afraid to touch it, thinking it might all come off in my hand. It didn't, so I began tentatively at the ends, gently brushing it out and working my way up. As I reached the matted part, it began coming out by the brushful. By the time I got it all brushed out, there wasn't much left.

I put on a scarf, grabbed my wig, and headed to see Sara Lou to have her show me again how to fit and put on the wig, because it had been about three weeks since I'd bought it. It fit differently with no hair than it had when I had tried it on over my hair. I also asked Sara Lou to trim off the last few strands of hair I had left. I told her they were the loyal hangers-on, and I didn't have the heart to cut them off since they had stuck with me to the end!

I used Carepages to post online status updates for anyone who wanted to follow my progress. This particular site does not exist anymore, but there are several others like it, and I highly recommend this means of keeping friends and loved ones informed on the latest updates. Friends and family can add comments as well. My entry on my Carepages that day was, "So very glad God had the hairs on my head numbered ... that will come in handy when He puts them back! 'Nuff said!"

When I first put my wig on, I took a picture of myself in it and texted it to my friend Beth. She showed it to her husband and son, who had known and been around me for years. She didn't tell them I had a wig on in the photo. Their reaction was, "So ... why are you showing us a picture of Cathy?" I loved that!

Some people never realized I had lost my hair. We go to a family reunion in Alabama most summers. I wore the wig to it at the end of July 2014. When we went back a year later, a relative said, "I like your haircut." When I said I hadn't cut it and that this was what had grown out since the previous October, I got the response to which I had become accustomed: "That was a wig?"

Then there was my friend Becky. I had lost my hair in May,

and she and I went to lunch in August. She was aware I'd lost my hair but had not seen me since I'd been in treatment. Her comment was, "Cathy, your hair has grown out so nicely!" Keep in mind that my wig was shoulder length, and this was three months into treatment.

I replied, "Becky, I don't know how fast your hair grows, but I didn't grow this in three months! My hair is actually about a half inch long at this point!"

"That's not yours?" she asked.

I said, "Oh, it's mine—I paid for it. But I take it off every night!"

Speaking of paying for it, I used my health savings account money to pay for the wig. I checked online to make sure it was allowed, and it was.

One day in September 2014, Derick and Jill came over to watch an Oklahoma State football game. I was cooking dinner, and just as I opened the oven, I remembered Sara Lou's warning to stay away from hot ovens when wearing a synthetic wig because the heat could melt the hairs. I ran to swap the wig for a headscarf.

Jill posted a picture later that day of me in my scarf, and one comment especially made me smile: "She lost her hair?"

I wondered when and how quickly my hair would grow back. It took a while to start, but by the time I went to Omaha in September 2014 for the stem cell transplant, I had about a half inch, enough to reassure myself that it would come back.

A stem cell transplant involves six days of hard chemo, and so I didn't have to wonder whether I would lose what I had managed to regrow so far. My fear was confirmed when I saw, on the list of things to bring, a lint roller. I knew exactly why that was on the list.

After the six days of chemo had the expected result, I used

the lint roller this time to take off my new "crop." It's hard to describe what that feels like, rolling a lint roller over your balding head. The hair came out completely this time, maybe because the new growth was not very strong to start with. "Chemo hairs," Sara Lou called them.

The second time my hair came out was October 2014. I didn't mind wearing the wig in the winter; it kept my head warm and covered my ears. I did have to remember to hang on to it on windy days though! I learned that one day after nearly having it blow off. I had visions of myself chasing it down the street and trying to stop it with my foot. What a sight that would have been!

By March 2015, my hair had grown out almost an inch, and the wig was starting to slip slide around. The weather had warmed up enough that I finally got brave enough to venture out without the wig. The first day was a Saturday in mid-March, and Ronnie and I went to a cow sale in Missouri where no one knew me. Coincidentally, this was the same sale we had gone to when I was first going through tests the year before.

The next day was Sunday—time to expose the new me to people who know and love me. It was just before Easter, which was important because it had been Easter morning the year before that I had stood before the same group and told them I had cancer. What a difference a year can make!

It was interesting to see people's reactions to my new look when I first began going without the wig. My one inch of hair was a lot to me, compared to the bald head that no one had seen under my wig. Looking back at pictures, though, it was still very short.

I especially loved my son Dan's comment on my somewhat

spiky hair. He said, "You look like a talk show host who should be sitting on a stool with a mug in your hand."

I told myself the first picture without the wig would be with my yet-to-be-born grandson, Israel, who was due the following week. I had to wait an extra two weeks for him to arrive, but after making sure my hair was longer than his, we had our picture. That picture graces the cover of the book in your hand.

CHAPTER 6

*I*n Sickne*ss* and in Health

Wednesday, May 14, was Ronnie's and my third wedding anniversary. The extent of our commemoration of the occasion was an appointment at HOG because I was still in isolation.

Later that night, in the wee hours I had chest pain so severe that I called 911. This was different from the a-fib I had had earlier; all I could think of was that it must be a heart attack. The EMTs came to the house, hooked me up to their monitors, and insisted my heart was in rhythm and all appeared normal. I kept asking them, "But why does it hurt so much?" They had no answer, and because there was nothing more for them to do, they left.

The following day, I had a scheduled appointment at the oncologist's office. I had been receiving Neupogen shots, which stimulate new blood cell production. Blood cells are produced in the bone marrow. Among other routine questions the nurse asked was, "Are you having any bone pain?"

They had told me earlier that the shots can cause bone pain, but I had imagined it to be in the long bones—arms, legs, and perhaps joints. Suddenly the light went on. I pointed to the center of my chest bone and asked her, "Could that pain be here?" She replied that the pain could indeed be in the sternum. I was both relieved to know it was not another problem with my heart and encouraged that there must have been a lot of blood cells produced during the night!

After the a-fib episode ten days earlier, the cardiologist had ordered a heart stress test. We had been told it could be six to seven weeks to get a spot on the schedule for this test, and so at the time we took what was available, which was July, and asked to be placed on a waiting list in case anything earlier became available. We were waiting for the elevator after a HOG appointment on May 15, and I was just about to take a sip of coffee that Ronnie had brought me when my phone rang. The voice on the other end of the line asked, "Have you had any coffee today?" They had had a cancellation for the next day, but the test required that I not have any caffeine for twenty-four hours!

My reply: "Not yet!" I quickly poured out the coffee and was able to have the test the following day, which was two months earlier than originally scheduled.

The week of May 19 was a busy one on the treatment calendar and included daily visits to HOG for chemo. New on this week's menu were pumps to be brought home and started or discontinued during the night, as well as eye drops to protect from yet another side effect of one of the drugs. But it did not include any hospital trips, which, according to my new definition of the word, made it somewhat "normal."

Speaking of normal, my job was such that I could work from anywhere that had a good Wi-Fi signal, but I would still try to go into my office to work when I could despite all the appointments. When asked, "What are you doing here?" I would always reply, "I needed some normal!"

However, even the new normal didn't last long. I will assume most everyone is aware of the more common side effects of chemo. On the Friday of Memorial Day weekend, I jumped up from the sofa to run to the bathroom. In doing so, I slipped on the wood floor, fell, and hit my head on the tile floor.

I didn't think much of it because I only had a slight cut to my left eyebrow. Ronnie was concerned because he said he heard my head hit the floor from across the room. I brushed off his concern and had only one thing on my mind at the moment. I got up and went on into the bathroom.

The next day, Saturday, May 24, I felt particularly listless. Ronnie's calendar note for the day said, "Extremely weak, slurred speech." I had an appointment to go in to Highlands (in Fayetteville because the Rogers office was not open on Saturdays) for a Neupogen shot anyway. Ronnie had to practically carry me to the car because I was so weak. It is about a forty-five-minute drive from our house, and all the way down there he couldn't understand anything I was saying.

When we got there, they brought out a wheelchair. While they wheeled me in, Ronnie called Aimee. When he described my symptoms, she suggested we ask for them to give me some intravenous fluids in addition to my scheduled shot, and if I was not better, I should go straight to the emergency room. They gave me two bags of fluids, but I was no better, and so Ronnie drove back to Rogers and directly to the hospital.

We sat in the waiting area of the emergency room for what seemed hours, even though it wasn't. I asked Ronnie to tell them that I could not put one foot in front of the other or put two words together in a sentence. I was eventually admitted. I didn't know what was wrong this time; we all thought I was suffering side effects from the four weeks of chemo.

What I thought would be just another couple of days in

the hospital turned into a week, then another week, and still another week. The chemo had obliterated my immune system. Blood was drawn and tested every day to see if my counts were starting back up.

Every day brought another disappointment. My nonexistent immune system had been replaced by a tangle of intravenous tubes leading to multiple hanging bags of antibiotics, antifungals, and antivirals. There were six or seven different things flowing in through my port during the three weeks I lay there waiting for my body to rebound. Due to the fall at home, I was labeled a fall risk and was not allowed to get up except to go to the bathroom (with assistance).

During these three weeks, I had three more episodes of a-fib and received eight units of blood and countless bags of platelets.

In addition to the aforementioned side effects, I had mouth sores and had lost my appetite. I continued to lose weight. During every night—why they do it then, I still don't know—an aide carried in a scale to weigh me. I dreaded seeing him walk in with the scale slung over his shoulder. I truly hated having to get on that thing.

I was determined to not drop below one hundred pounds; I am five feet seven inches tall. I managed to stop the downward slide eventually at 102 pounds, a total loss from the beginning of my illness of 41 pounds, or 28 percent of my body weight. The Neupogen shots I had been receiving almost daily had initially been given in my belly, injected into my muffin top. By June 3, even that was gone.

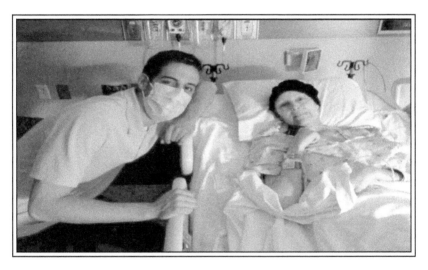

Derick, Jill, and Dan came by the
hospital every chance they got.

CHAPTER 7
Get Me to the Church on Time

Anyone who knows me will tell you I am *not* superstitious. Having said that, on Friday, June 13, eight days prior to Derick and Jill's wedding, Ronnie left the hospital to go get a haircut, mow the lawn, and take a shower. Because he would never leave me alone, he had asked Cindy, our friend Joe's wife, to sit with me.

I fell asleep, and it is at this point I must rely on what others have told me happened.

I am told I woke up speaking nonsense. Cindy called Hannah, the charge nurse on duty, who called Dr. Travis. Two MRIs and a CT scan were done. The radiologist could see something in my brain, but it could not be determined whether it was bleeding or an infection. Either one was life-threatening because I had no platelets to clot blood and no white blood cells to fight infection.

Dr. Travis had me immediately transported by helicopter to Washington Regional, a hospital in Fayetteville, about fifteen miles away. There, a neurosurgeon waited, anticipating surgery would be required regardless of what the problem turned out to be.

As soon as Ronnie arrived at Washington Regional, the

surgeon questioned him about the events of the past month. When Ronnie mentioned that I had fallen and hit my head, the doctor smiled. He said he had suspected the shadow on my brain could be old blood, and if he had to put a timeline on it, he would have guessed it was about three weeks old. My fall had been three weeks prior, to the day.

For some reason, the bleeding had started again that day, and according to the numbers and science, specifically physiology, I should not have been able to clot blood. My platelet count was essentially nonexistent.

Still, the bleeding in my brain stopped.

I also had a high fever but couldn't be given anything for that due to the risk of bleeding. The first thing I remember after arriving at Washington Regional is a fan blowing on me. It was so cold, I'm not even sure I had a sheet over me; they were trying to bring down the fever. I don't recall seeing anything or anyone in that ICU room, but sensing someone near me, I do remember saying, "I will give you anything to turn that fan off of me!"

I think that was the point everyone else realized I was going to pull through.

The following day, Saturday, June 14, was one week before the wedding. It was also Ronnie's birthday. I remember Don, a friend from church, bringing Ronnie a birthday cake because it had strawberries on top that I couldn't eat. (Remember, fresh fruit and flowers were forbidden due to the possibility of germs.) Our friend Pam brought donuts and a pot of coffee to the "party."

I was in ICU four days and finally moved to a regular room on Wednesday, June 18, three days prior to the wedding.

Every day a parade of specialists came through my room—cardiologist, infectious disease specialist, neurologist, nutritionist, physical therapist, and of course one of the oncologists from HOG. Every day I told each of them, "I *have* to be out of here by Saturday!"

The day I moved out of ICU, Ronnie brought the dress I was going to wear to the wedding to hang in my room. That long, dark dress hanging on the door in the shadows gave the nurses and aides a start every time they entered the room at night! It encouraged and inspired me, however, and was a very visible reminder to everyone entering the room that I fully intended to leave on Saturday!

June 20, 2014, was a Friday, the day before the wedding, just a week after the helicopter ride and brain surgery that didn't happen. I had a low-grade infection, and doctors determined the source might be the chemo port. The decision was made to take it out.

To do that, an IV had to be started. Due to my emaciated state, it took two and a half hours of sticking me to finally find a vein. Each person could only attempt three sticks, and then he or she would find someone else to try. Finally, an ultrasound machine was used to locate a vein.

All the time they were trying to insert the IV, I was watching Derick, Jill, and Dan at the wedding rehearsal on closed-circuit TV on my laptop. I had planned the rehearsal dinner during the weeks of isolation at home. The menu was brisket (my late husband Rick's recipe) and barbecue chicken, with a western theme.

Ronnie had gotten me a pink checked western shirt and western belt with silver hearts on it to wear to the rehearsal and dinner. My friend Pam had bought me a denim skirt because I had lost so much weight I had no jeans that would fit. All of us were holding out hope that I might be able to go at the last minute.

It was not to be.

I knew didn't have the strength to go to both the rehearsal and the wedding. Of course I chose the wedding. Dan, along with Rick's brother, Mike, and his family represented our side of the family at the rehearsal dinner. Dan gave a speech that brought me to tears when I heard it later.

The day of the wedding finally arrived. A friend from church had applied polish to my nails the day before. While sitting in bed that morning and putting on makeup for the first time in six weeks, I realized I was green from the neck up thanks to the antiseptic used during the port removal procedure the previous day. I called an aide to my room and pleaded, "Help! I *can't* be green!" She helped me scrub off the stain of the antiseptic using the tiny little alcohol swabs used for shots.

I had not put on anything other than a hospital gown since entering the first hospital on May 24, almost a month before. I also had not had on my mother-of-the-groom dress since the wedding planning meeting the evening of the day I was first diagnosed.

As I slipped into the dress, I couldn't help but think of all that had happened since I'd last tried it on. It was quite loose this time, but by some small miracle I had chosen a style that was a loose drape as opposed to a more fitted style. I had bought the dress right after Derick proposed, before I knew I was sick.

The wedding was at 2:00. Derick and Jill had told me on the phone earlier that morning that if I left the hospital at noon, I would be there in plenty of time because the church was only a few minutes away.

The hospital staff told me I was the first patient to ever leave the hospital in a formal gown! I had borrowed a silver wrap at the last minute to cover all the bruises on my arms from having been stuck so much the day before.

I was in a wheelchair and on oxygen, but with a *lot* of help, I was finally on my way to the wedding. Given that I had been in bed four weeks straight and had lost so much weight, I could barely walk.

Derick had pushed an empty wheelchair down the aisle in rehearsal, still not knowing for sure whether I would be there the next day. I had worked with the physical therapist at the hospital, practicing walking, determined that I would walk down that aisle. But when I saw how long it was and the slope I would have to walk to get back up it, I let Derick push me in the wheelchair for the wedding.

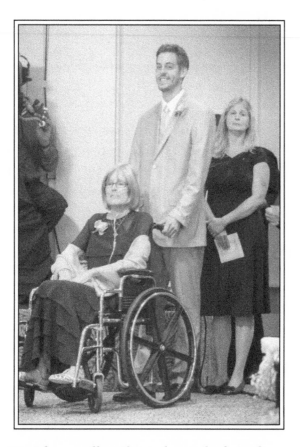

Derick was all smiles as he pushed me down
the aisle at his wedding. I was 102 pounds and
on oxygen in this photo. Pam, ever-vigilant as
my nurse for the day, was right behind us.

My friend Pam, the same one who'd bought the skirt, is also a surgical nurse. She volunteered to accompany me at the wedding to help Ronnie care for me and convey to people that they could not get close to me because my immune system was still compromised. She arrived at the church before we did and disinfected the room where I would wait before the wedding began. Without knowing what I was wearing, she had on a dress the same color as mine!

As soon as we arrived, the wedding planners explained the order of service during the ceremony. I don't remember exactly what the original plan was, only that it involved me lighting a candle. Thankfully Pam was paying attention and announced, "She can't be near a candle—she's on oxygen. We'd blow up the building!"

The wedding was beautiful. Dan was best man, of course. We had a lot of family and friends there who had driven from out of state; I hated not being able to hug or even visit with them. I wondered whether some of them made the trip thinking they might not see me again. I am thankful it was captured on video and that there were a lot of pictures taken because I didn't get to stay long after the ceremony. I did see Derick and Jill cut the cake at the reception but I did not have the strength to stay after that.

After the wedding, Ronnie and I went by the pharmacy, where we had asked the hospital to call in the prescriptions I would continue taking at home. The pharmacy was closed, and so Ronnie took me home, leaving me in the care of his cousin Sheryl. After calling the hospital to have the prescriptions called in to a different pharmacy, he left to go pick them up.

I was exhausted. I pulled off the wig and dropped to the couch, still in my dress.

CHAPTER 8

The Ahh of the Storm

Upon determining the extent of my disease just after diagnosis, Dr. Travis had told me it could take four to six cycles, twenty-eight days each, of chemo, which meant repeating the one I had completed just before I fell a month earlier. Even aside from the fall, I had barely survived the first round of treatment.

June 26, five days after the wedding, was the date selected to scan to see how much of the cancer had been eradicated after the first four-week cycle, and to make a plan for future treatment.

We were all amazed, Dr. Travis included, when these first scans came back completely clear! We were overwhelmed and so grateful to Dr. Travis for his expertise. Ronnie told him, "Cathy and I both believe that all healing ultimately comes from God, whether it's instantaneous miraculous healing or through medical procedures. We thank God that He led you into medicine, that He gave you the discipline to complete your studies, and that you had twenty-six years of experience prior to her case given that it's been such a difficult one."

Dr. Travis and his nurse, Anne, are an amazing team. I still see them every three to six months.

I had left the hospital in a wheelchair and on oxygen. Encouraged by the clear scans just five days later, my goals were to get off the oxygen and get back on my feet. Dr. Travis wanted me to work up to walking 1,500 feet per day.

Ronnie mapped a fifty-foot route through the house and was relentless as a trainer, walking with me as I pushed a borrowed walker. He also kept meticulous records of my walks, plus additional spreadsheets, one each for my temperature, blood oxygen (we bought a finger monitor), what food I ate, and my weight.

At my lowest, I had lost 41 pounds, or 28 percent of my body weight. Who knew it would be so hard to put it back on? It was summer, and I came to hate those weight-loss commercials on TV; I would grab the remote and mute them. I had never noticed there were so many of them!

I was about four weeks into my recuperation when I received a video chat call on Sunday afternoon, July 20, from Derick and Jill. "Guess what? You're going to be a grandma!" I was speechless—thrilled, but speechless! Now I had even more inspiration to recuperate and recover.

After the month at home, I was ready to return to work, which I did on July 22. I had been working from the hospital as I could and from home, but this was my first day back in the office.

I had gained almost eight pounds in the month at home and I was still a little wobbly on my feet, but it felt great to be able to walk back into the office. Ironically, this was the week Ronnie and I would have been on the cruise that my boss had given us the previous Christmas. We missed the cruise, but I was thrilled to be coming back to work.

The last weekend of July was an annual family reunion in Alabama. So many of my extended family had followed my progress on Carepages and prayed for me. It meant the world to me to be able to make this trip and thank them in person.

I had been back to work about a month when I e-mailed Dr. Travis's nurse, Anne, to let her know I had not felt well for several days. Dr. Travis ordered CT and PET scans, which were scheduled for the next day, August 26. Scans were scheduled for 3:00, and Dr. Travis had the results before 5:00.

The scans were still clear! It had been exactly two months since the first clear scan.

CHAPTER 9

Omaha? Nebraska?

I had been thrilled when the first post-treatment scan in June indicated the cancer was eradicated. I thought I was done— we had beat it! Now I could truly get back to the original normal.

Imagine my surprise when, at my next visit, Dr. Travis told me he wanted me to go to Omaha for a stem cell transplant. My response was, "Omaha? Nebraska? For a what? Why?"

Remember, I don't like surprises.

As it turns out, Nebraska Medicine in Omaha is described by some as the equivalent of M. D. Anderson or Mayo Clinic when it comes to treatment of Lymphoma. When Dr. Travis first mentioned it, I pictured Nebraska being well north and Omaha being in the far western reaches of the state. I was pleasantly surprised to learn Omaha is about seven hours due north from where I live. Kansas City is about halfway between here and there. I had been to Kansas City, that made Omaha seem closer.

A stem cell transplant candidate needs to be in remission to be eligible for the process, because it is not an actual transplant in the truest sense of the word. Rather, it is a harvesting of one's own healthy stem cells (immature blood cells). Once an adequate number of the cells is collected, the cells are frozen. After six days of aggressive chemotherapy they are thawed out, and put back into the patient. The recovery is much quicker with this fresh influx of healthy cells, and there is no chance of rejection because they are the patient's own cells.

About the time I went back to work in July, we started the preliminary work and eventually scheduled our first trip to Omaha for later in August, to meet and be evaluated by Dr. Julie Vose. Dr. Travis had told me of her expertise in this field, but I subsequently learned that she was also the chief of the oncology department at Nebraska Medicine, and at the time she was the president of the American Society of Clinical Oncology. I was indeed in good hands!

Our first appointment to meet her was on August 28, two days after my second clear scan. She and my case manager, Stacy, were extremely helpful and patient in answering our myriad questions about the transplant procedure, especially my concerns about whether the transplant was absolutely necessary.

My major concern was the time involved. We were told the entire process would require anywhere from three to five weeks in Omaha. Dr. Vose explained that the stem cell transplant could reduce my chance of recurrence from 70 percent down to just 30 percent. That put the time required into perspective for me, and I was convinced it was indeed necessary.

By the end of August, I felt so good physically that I was determined my stay would be on the short end of the three- to five-week range. Once Dr. Vose agreed I was a candidate for the transplant, we had to wait for insurance to approve it. As with any major medical procedure, this would be very expensive.

Once that approval was received, we scheduled our return trip to Omaha for September 22.

We spent the first three weeks of September getting ready to be gone from home for possibly a month or more, if necessary. I had to get things caught up at work, although my job is such that I could do a lot remotely. We had the newspaper stopped and the mail forwarded. Fortunately, it was the time of year that we could simply turn off the heat and air conditioning. I took my house plants to the office so they could be looked after. We let the neighbors know what the plan was so they would know we hadn't moved!

Dan, Derick, and Jill came over the day before we left to help with last-minute preparations; we emptied out the refrigerator and sent perishables home with them.

CHAPTER 10

Transplanted

We made the seven-hour drive to Omaha on Monday, September 22, stopping in Kansas City for lunch. We had packed my Pontiac Vibe to the brim, taking anything and everything we thought we might need for a month's stay.

Upon arriving about 4:00, we unloaded the car, hauling everything up to our fourth-floor room. We explored what would be our home for the next several weeks, and then found a local place to eat, knowing that I would soon be confined within the walls of the transplant center.

Nebraska Medicine had a facility at the time that allowed us to stay in the same building in which I would be receiving treatment, even though I was considered an outpatient until the actual chemo treatment began. Ronnie stayed in the two-room suite with me as my caregiver. This made it seem much less like the hospital rooms in which I had already spent so many days and nights that year. Ronnie would be able to sleep in a bed instead of the recliner in which he had spent thirty-three nights!

Tuesday was primarily consumed with administrative tasks. We met with Stacy, my case manager whom we had met at the first appointment a month before. We then completed the registration process with another lady named Jamie. The day included a meeting with Karen for a pharmacy review. (As my caretaker, Ronnie would be responsible for giving me pills each day, as well as monitoring my weight, vitals, intake, and output). Karen explained that the pills for each twenty-four-hour period would be delivered to our room each evening. These pills were my routine daily prescriptions, supplements as well as medication for pain, if requested.

JoAnn gave us a tour of the facilities, showing us the apheresis room, where the stem cells would be harvested, and the treatment rooms, where I would go twice a day most days for all chemo treatments and transfusions.

I am able to include all the various names because Ronnie kept precise notes on all meetings and treatments throughout the year. I am so thankful for his meticulous attention to detail!

Besides the meetings with these four people, on Tuesday I also had blood drawn along with a chest X-ray and EKG.

Wednesday's schedule included an echocardiogram (chemo is hard on the heart), more administrative details, and a meeting with Dr. Vose. Ronnie's notes showed my weight was up to 122 pounds with clothes and shoes.

On Thursday I resumed the Neupogen shots to stimulate the growth of stem cells, which would be collected the following week.

Finally, on Friday I once again had surgery, this time to insert a two-way catheter into the opposite side of my chest from where the chemo port had been. This one was similar to those used for dialysis, with two tubes extending from it, one for the blood to be drawn out and the other for the blood to reenter my body.

Monday was the day the harvest was to begin—that's

what they call the extraction of the stem cells. We had been told that harvesting could take one to four days. Things had been moving along quickly and proceeding right on schedule. I was feeling good, eating well, and gaining weight. I was determined that my harvest would be on the shorter end of that range.

Imagine my disappointment when, after having been there a week already, the morning blood draw revealed there were not enough stem cells to even attempt to harvest that day. This possibility had been presented earlier, but I had not paid much attention.

In this situation, there is another shot, Plerixafor, that is given to supercharge the production of stem cells. I received this shot Monday evening and went to bed praying that the shot would work.

Tuesday's predawn blood draw did indeed bring good news! We went downstairs and reported to the apheresis room, where the harvesting takes place, at 7:00 a.m. Within the hour, I was hooked up to a dialysis-like machine with my blood flowing into it, passing through a centrifuge to extract the stem cells, and reentering my body. I was hooked up to the machine till almost 1:00 p.m. that day, after which we went to get lunch and then headed back to our room to await the the call that would tell us count of cells that were gathered that day.

When we got the call with the count, it was good but not great. We would be going back the following day. In addition to receiving another Plerixafor shot, that afternoon also included a transfusion of platelets.

This was to be the routine Tuesday, Wednesday, and Thursday: Neupogen shot, harvest for five hours in the morning, go to lunch, wait for the call with the count, and

Plerixafor shot and platelets in the afternoon. After Thursday's harvest, we were told that if the count still was not high enough on Friday, we might have to go home.

We sent out calls for more prayers.

On Friday we again reported to the apheresis room. By this time we were on a first name basis with everyone in there, both other patients and the nurses who operated the machines. They knew as well as we did that regardless of the day's result, this would be our last day with them.

I still don't understand how they count the cells or even how to interpret the number that represents how many cells have been collected. I remember wondering, if we didn't reach the required number that day, what they would do with the ones already harvested.

As it turned out, I didn't have to worry about any of that. It had taken four days, but finally I had (barely) cleared the minimum amount needed. We would be staying to complete the transplant!

Having been an outpatient up to this point, now that chemo was to begin, I was admitted. That meant we had to move to a different floor. Ronnie wouldn't let me help and spent the afternoon hauling all our stuff to the new room.

That same night, October 3, was the first of six days of chemo, ending on October 9. That is the day that is now my transplant "birthday," because October 9 was the day of the actual transplant, when my stem cells were infused back into me. The transplant center has a custom of having a little celebration with a birthday cake being brought in and singing! More important, it is the date from which my survival milestones are counted.

Because it had taken four days of harvesting to accumulate enough stem cells, there were fourteen bags of them, and it took two days to put them back in. The cells arrived in the treatment room after I was already there.

The cells had been frozen during the six days of chemo, and they arrived on a rolling cart accompanied by two young men. I watched as one of the young men turned a bag of my hard-earned cells over and over in his hands to thaw them. After all, they couldn't exactly be heated in the microwave!

Due to the volume of cells being infused back into me, I received intravenous fluids along with the cells and also through the night between the two days of transplant. Our dear friends Joe and Cindy had made the seven-hour trip to Omaha and were with us for both transplant days and the day after.

The transplant days were Thursday and Friday, October 9–10. I got a really sore throat over the weekend, but no mouth sores this time due to the fact that they had me suck on popsicles to constrict the blood vessels in my mouth and keep the chemo drugs from causing the sores.

Ronnie, ever the faithful caregiver, let me rest over the weekend. But starting Monday, October 13, he was back in drill sergeant mode! He followed the instructions to the letter, making sure I got up, showered, dressed, and brushed my teeth every morning. He once again logged the laps I walked—up and down the hallway this time.

During the two weeks following the transplant, I received three units of blood and ten bags of platelets. It is understandable that Ronnie's entry in his calendar on October 24 was, finally, "No blood products!"

It was halfway through this two-week recovery period that I had a very special visitor. Derick and Jill had let us know that on October 18, they would reveal the gender of their baby—my first grandchild. I was hovering near my laptop with my phone in hand, not knowing whether the news would come via phone call or live video chat, when in walked Dan! I was still in such a brain fog from the chemo that it didn't occur to me to wonder why he was there or how he'd gotten there. I simply invited him over to my laptop to hear the call with me.

He stood there for a moment, waiting for me to notice the bouquet of flowers with a blue balloon attached that he was holding. What I hadn't realized was that Dan was the deliverer of the news I had been awaiting! We were both on the video call and had a good laugh with Derick and Jill immediately after I realized what was happening.

I was thrilled to learn I would have a grandson, but hugging Dan was the best medicine I had during the whole time in Omaha. In fact, after not having been out of the room for an entire week except to walk up and down the hall, I was able to give him a short tour of the facility that night.

Dan had to leave early the next morning. I suppose I overextended myself because Ronnie's calendar entry the following day was, "Slept all day," and the entry two days later was, "Started to wake up."

On Saturday, October 25, I was finally released back to outpatient status, which meant we moved back to the fourth floor where we had been before the chemo had begun on October 9. Ronnie once again hauled all of our stuff, which had somehow grown, to our third room since our stay there.

The best part about being outpatient was that I could leave the building. The following day was Sunday. We went to church and out to lunch with our friends Joe and Regina. It felt so good to be outside!

On Monday, October 27, I received my last bag of platelets. I had received three prior to the transplant, ten during the two weeks after, and this one made fourteen. Dr. Vose had said after my brain bleed that they were not going to take a chance on my platelets falling too low, and they certainly didn't!

On Tuesday we got the best news of all—well, second to Dan's visit. We would finally be going home the following day!

The catheter that had been inserted into my chest more than a month earlier was removed the morning of the day we were leaving. The doctor who removed it was not thrilled that we planned to start home immediately and be on the road for seven hours. He cautioned us to find a hospital if the site started bleeding. Still determined to leave, we assured him we would.

We had spent thirty-eight days in Omaha. It was October 29. I will always remember that the Royals were in the World Series that year, and the date of the final game on this day. The Series was tied three games apiece with the tiebreaker game being played that night. I remember because the game was in Kansas City, and we had to drive through that crazy game traffic. The Royals lost.

CHAPTER 11
The Funny Stories I Can Share

No matter how serious a situation, I have always managed to keep my sense of humor. Even through this seemingly never-ending year of my life, there were always lighter moments sprinkled throughout. Here are just a few.

Before I was diagnosed, Ronnie had gotten the accompaniment disc for the song "I've Just Seen Jesus" for us to practice. The first week I was in the hospital, we had a good laugh when I said I didn't think it was a good idea to practice that song in a hospital room!

While in the hospital for chemo the last week of April, I was hooked up to a heart monitor that was monitored constantly by a team two floors below my room. During a visit from a friend, I was sharing with her the passage from the Bible in 2 Kings about Hezekiah being told by Isaiah that Hezekiah would die, then petitioning God for his life, and God granting him fifteen more years.

I got excited, I guess, because Greg, my nurse, poked his head in the room to see what was going on. I had apparently gotten worked up enough that it had set off the heart monitors! I already knew Greg was a fellow believer, and he understood why I got so excited about that passage.

Probably the funniest thing was during the gravest crisis, the airlift from one hospital to another due to the brain bleed. I don't recall being put on the helicopter or taken off, but during the ride I remembered opening my eyes and realizing I was in the air.

In my addled state of mind, I somehow thought we were flying to the East Coast. I didn't know where on the East Coast or why, but that was where I thought we were headed. Ronnie is a private pilot, and I somehow had the idea that he would try to rent a plane and follow us! I remember thinking I had to find a way to stop him.

Even after we landed at the second hospital and they were getting me situated in a room in ICU, I recall thinking, *I don't know why they're going to all this trouble. We'll be leaving again in the morning.* I still had in my mind that we would be continuing to the East Coast.

Ronnie tells me I woke two different times during that night to make sure he knew we weren't going to the East Coast! He had no idea what I was talking about at that point but assured me we weren't going to the East Coast.

Recently, we were somewhere—I don't recall where—and someone mentioned the East Coast. We both looked at each other with the same thought: "We're not going there!"

The day after the helicopter ride was a Saturday. Dr. Travis was not on duty or on call, but I think he wanted to see for himself that I was still alive, and so he came by the hospital. He had been repairing a fence and he was not dressed anything like I was used to seeing. I was still a little out of it, and somehow I thought he was a plumber who had come to make a repair in my room!

When I left the hospital, or rather hospitals, after the three weeks I spent in one and a week in another, I was on oxygen.

A man from the home health service would come twice a week to deliver new canisters and pick up the empty ones. Every time he came, I was on the couch, and he would wave to me from the front door. After four weeks of this routine, I went back to work, reminding Ronnie to call the home health company to have the equipment picked up.

The same guy came to retrieve the equipment, and when he didn't see me on the couch, he told Ronnie, "I'm so sorry for your loss."

After glancing over all the tanks, tubes, and equipment he had gathered, Ronnie asked, "What did I lose?"

The young man said, "Your wife!"

Ronnie replied, "I didn't lose her—I know where she is."

The guy asked, "Is she resting?"

Ronnie said, "No, she's at work!"

He told Ronnie that he had never picked up oxygen equipment from a patient who had been on as high a level as I was who had survived. I would love to have seen his face!

Ronnie's cousin Sheryl is like a sister to him. She came from Oklahoma for Derick's wedding and then stayed a few days to help us. She and her son Chris stayed in a local hotel but came over several afternoons to clean our house.

She did some shopping while she was here, and knowing I had lost so much weight, she wanted to get me something I could wear till I put some weight back on. She decided I couldn't be any bigger than a size two and bought me some jeans. I didn't have the energy to try them on until several days after she left.

I tried pulling them on while lying on the bed. They were skinny jeans, and even in my emaciated state, I could not get into them. Not for lack of trying, mind you—Ronnie even tried to shake me into them! I was laughing so hard, partly from the hilarious sight of us trying to get them on and partly from joy that they were too small.

During the month after the wedding, before I went back to work, I was recovering at home. When I wasn't making laps through the house with the walker, I was on the couch. I did not have my taste buds back yet but wanted to eat. It is really hard to describe, but whatever it was, I satisfied it by copying pages and pages of recipes! I remember one in particular was for mashed potatoes, of all things. As I recall, it was for a large amount of mashed potatoes!

As my appetite came back, Ronnie was thrilled when I would crave something in particular. He would not let me in the kitchen, though, still determined he would take care of me. A couple of things I thought sounded good were very simple to prepare—or so I thought. The problem is Ronnie does not cook.

Imagine the scene: me reclining on the couch in one room, shouting directions into the kitchen on how to boil water for spaghetti or poached eggs, starting with where the pan was located!

I'll share one more story. I recall during the three weeks spent on my back before the helicopter ride, telling the nurses, "I'm tall. You'll see! When I get better, I will come walking back in here. I will have my wig on, my contact lenses in, makeup on, and be dressed in real clothes. You won't recognize me!"

That very thing did come to pass. Ronnie and I went back to the hospital in September to pick up copies of scans to take to Omaha. As we walked down the hall, one of my nurses, Carol, was sitting at her station in the hallway. She glanced at me and looked back down at her paperwork. As we got closer, she looked up again, this time catching sight of

Ronnie. As soon as she recognized him, her eyes cut to me, and she started crying.

She had been one of the nurses telling Ronnie the day I left the hospital via helicopter three months earlier that she was sorry. She and the others had not expected me to survive. On this day, she thanked us over and over for coming back to share the good news that I had survived. Apparently it is rare for patients to return after having recovered. She was so happy we had come to find her.

And I was so happy to be there to thank her!

CHAPTER 12

*P*rayer—*The Greater Work*

Prayer has been the key to my miraculous healing. Even my doctor is amazed I lived.

I was asked at what point I realized I was going to survive the cancer. The answer is, "From the beginning!"

Shortly after I was diagnosed, Beth, who is my friend and my pastor's wife, sent me a prayer from a Bible study we were doing at the time. She was further along in it than I was, and so I hadn't yet seen this prayer. I don't recall the prayer itself, but embedded within the prayer was a Bible reference, Psalm 118:17. I looked it up, and it read, "I shall not die, but live, and declare the works of the Lord."

I knew when I read that verse that I would not die. I just knew! If you have experienced God speaking to you through His word, the Bible, you know what I mean.

I didn't know just how close I would come to dying, but God assured me through that verse that I would indeed live. I know the prayers of so many played a big part in God healing me.

One of the first prayers that was a factor in my survival was actually in the Bible. Just days after the beginning of this journey, God brought to my mind King Hezekiah's prayer in 2 Kings 20.

Isaiah had told the king to prepare to die, but Hezekiah called out to God, reminding Him of Hezekiah's faithfulness and asking for more time. Verse 5 says, "I have heard your prayer, I have seen your tears, surely I will heal you." God kept bringing me across words of healing.

On the Sunday night after the first week of chemo, after waking up at home at 2:00 a.m. with my heart in atrial fibrillation, on the way to the emergency room I knew no one would be awake to text for prayer. I asked God to wake up a prayer warrior to pray.

I learned a couple of days later that it was our friend Don who got the wake-up call from God and answered faithfully! This is the same Don who brought Ronnie the birthday pie with the strawberries. Thank you, Don, for the pie and the prayer!

My boss, Paul, was in India on a mission trip during my initial treatment. Ramesh is a pastor there, and he and his wife, Esther, are godly prayer warriors. Paul sent me a video of Ramesh praying for me from India. When you hear him pray, it's obvious he has "gotten hold" of God! I saved it of course, and it still brings me to tears when I watch it.

I was well aware my church family prayed for me. Many sent texts, cards, e-mails, Carepages messages, and phone calls to say they were praying. It brought me to tears to learn that one Wednesday night, they devoted the entire weekly prayer meeting to pray for me. I later found out that some fasted as well.

My friend Donna, who lives in Louisiana, let me know that her church, North Monroe Baptist, was praying for me. A local friend, Linda, shared that her small group at First

Baptist Church Bentonville, Arkansas, were praying as well. Another friend whose husband teaches life skills in a prison told me his students were praying for me. Some of them sent cards, and those made me cry. Other churches praying were Monte Ne Baptist here in Rogers, nearby Bella Vista Baptist, and Eagle Heights Baptist in Stillwater, Oklahoma, where Derick attended while in college. My humble, eternal thanks to all of you!

One more prayer stands out to me. Shortly after I got out of the hospital, on one of my first ventures out, a lady we didn't know stopped Ronnie and me in a parking lot and asked if she could pray for me. I was not wearing my wig and hadn't added much to the 102 pounds after I'd left the hospital, and so I'm sure it was obvious that I was in the middle of a cancer battle.

This godly woman walked up to us with no hesitation and asked if she could pray for me. She could have been an angel for all I know. I decided then and there I was going to make a point to be on the lookout for people who needed prayer and follow her practice.

That so many people prayed for me means more to me than I can begin to say, and I am a better prayer warrior because I now know in a very personal way what a difference prayer makes!

Now, when people ask me to pray for them, I pray then and there. I pray scripture back to God and over others. I put my hands on them or on their pictures. I pray with faith, believing and knowing firsthand what God can do!

Recently I saw something that spoke to me: "We don't pray for the greater works, prayer IS the greater work!"

Derick, Jill, Pastor Scott, Pam, Ronnie, and I
pray just before Derick and Jill's wedding.

CHAPTER 13

The Power of the Word

When I refer to the Bible as God's word, I mean that in the most literal sense. Over my fifty-plus years as a follower of Jesus, the Bible is the way He most often communicates with me. Following are a few of the specific verses through which He spoke to me throughout this cancer journey. I have used many of these to encourage others going through similar illnesses.

First and foremost, the verse that was embedded in the prayer shared with me by my friend Beth: Psalm 118:17. "I shall not die, but live, and declare the works of the Lord." I said before and will continue to say it is when I read this verse that I first knew I would survive. Now I am fulfilling the second part of that verse, declaring His works in me!

Our friends Donnie and Debbie prayed over me and shared this scripture: Isaiah 41:10. "Fear not, for I am with you; Be not dismayed, for I am your God. I will strengthen you, Yes, I will help you, I will uphold you with My righteous right hand." There are thousands of promises in the Bible. I clung to this one in the darkest of nights.

I mentioned earlier that I had a peace from the start about dying, if indeed that were to be the outcome of all of this. Philippians 1:19–26 spoke to me and put that peace into words.

> For I know that this will turn out for my deliverance through your prayer and the supply of the Spirit of Jesus Christ, according to my earnest expectation and hope that in nothing I shall be ashamed, but with all boldness, as always, so now also Christ will be magnified in my body, whether by life or by death. For to me, to live is Christ, and to die is gain. But if I live on in the flesh, this will mean fruit from my labor; yet what I shall choose I cannot tell. For I am hard-pressed between the two, having a desire to depart and be with Christ, which is far better. Nevertheless to remain in the flesh is more needful for you. *And being confident of this, I know that I shall remain and continue with you all* for your progress and joy of faith, that your rejoicing for me may be more abundant in Jesus Christ by my coming to you again. (Emphasis mine)

I have mentioned it twice already, but when you read it, I know you'll understand why this verse was so powerful for me. In 2 Kings 20:5, the prophet Isaiah tells Hezekiah, "Thus says the Lord ... 'I have heard your prayer, I have seen your tears; surely I will heal you.'"

Many verses were posted on my Carepages site. One verse posted there by my dear and longtime friend Tosh was Isaiah 43:2. "When you pass through the waters, I will be with you; And through the rivers, they shall not overflow you. When you walk through the fire, you shall not be burned."

This verse was such a comfort when I became overwhelmed at times.

The funniest verse anyone sent came from the children at church, on a poster they made. Micah 4:2 reads in the New King James translation, "But to you who fear My name the Sun of Righteousness shall arise with healing in His wings; and you shall go out and grow fat like stall-fed calves." They had heard I was struggling to eat!

These are all verses I had read before, most of them many times, but they practically jumped off the page as the Holy Spirit drew me to them and used them to speak to my heart.

We can never presume to know what God will do in any situation, but neither can we ever go wrong sharing scripture or encouraging others to read the scripture for themselves.

If you happen to be in a hospital room, there is almost always a Bible in the drawer of the nightstand!

CHAPTER 14

Miracles

Some people don't believe in miracles. I have been made explicitly aware of this recently by the replies to my online social media posts regarding the miraculous nature of my cancer milestones.

I believe in miracles for two reasons. First and foremost, because I believe in God—and not just any god but the God of the Bible, where we read of so many miracles.

I have no reason to believe God has changed; in fact, that is one of His characteristics: He does not change (Hebrews 13:8). Why would the God who did the miracles of the Bible not still do miracles today? I believe He can; it's simply that in Western society, we rely on so many things other than Him.

Second, I have experienced His miracles. Some people have told me I was lucky, or that these were simply coincidences, or it was the result of medical treatment. That might be the case if you were to look at them individually, but seeing them all together, it's obvious they weren't coincidences.

I did have excellent medical treatment, but not all of the miracles were medical in nature. I think after reading them here, you will agree they were indeed amazing works of God! Even the doctors agreed. Dr. Travis told me later he had not expected me to survive the helicopter ride. As mentioned in an earlier chapter, I had a brain bleed and a fever. Not only did I have no platelets to clot blood, but I also didn't have any white blood cells to fight the infection that caused the fever. And yet the bleeding stopped, and the infection subsided.

Dr. Travis asked us much later if we had ever heard the term *hanging crepe*. We had not. He explained that back in olden days, when there was an impending death within a household, the family would hang black crepe outside the house as a means of communicating the gravity of the situation to neighbors. He then went on to say, regarding my situation, that "there had been a lot of crepe hung that night" because no one expected me to live. Even after I left on the helicopter, as Ronnie and Cindy were packing up our belongings from three weeks in the first hospital, the nurses were telling him, "We're so sorry!"

Dr Travis told me initially that the aggressive treatment would consist of four to six cycles of a month-long regimen. I had started round one on April 28, reentered the hospital on May 24 after falling the day before, and left the hospital on June 21. On June 26, scans showed the cancer was gone! I was told it was doubtful I could have survived another cycle, much less four or five more rounds.

I was asked shortly after diagnosis what my pain level was, on a scale of one to ten. I asked where the pain would be. The nurse gave me an unbelieving look and then responded, "You should be wracked with pain! You really don't have any pain?" The only pain I had all year was the pain in my sternum the one night, which was a side effect of the Neupogen shots, and of course the mouth sores.

It is common knowledge that the hospital is the last place to go if you want to avoid catching something. Of the twenty-one days I was in the first hospital, nine days I had a white blood cell count of 0.0, and the following eight days it was 0.1. Yet I did not contract anything contagious.

As mentioned earlier, not all the miracles were medical related or necessarily have anything to do with me directly.

It occurred to us early on that it was surely no coincidence that within our small church of less than one hundred people, years before God had placed four people who were uniquely equipped and positioned close at hand to help in our situation. The first is Joe, who was not only a recently retired pharmaceutical salesman but, as mentioned previously, had specialized in oncology drugs. Cindy, his wife, is a med tech. She had recently taken partial retirement, which meant she happened to be available to sit with me the day I left the hospital on the helicopter. Aimee was a nurse at HOG who happened to be friends with Dr. Travis's nurse. Pam is a surgical nurse who listened to that still, small voice telling her to accompany me at the wedding. God had them right where they needed to be for Him to use them to play a part in saving my life. (I think of Pam every time I light a candle now!)

Here's another instance of a nonmedical miracle. In 2012 and 2013, Ronnie had worked at our farm in Oklahoma, growing hay. This involved almost weekly trips from spring through fall, staying several days each time. In the fall of 2013, six months before my diagnosis, he decided to lease the farm for the next year to his cousin. Unbeknownst to Ronnie at the time, this made it possible for him to be with me throughout the entire ordeal without having to worry about the farm. He stayed with me day and night, leaving only to go home to shower and change clothes, and then only when he had someone to sit with me.

Speaking of which, another little miracle happened during

one of these instances. On June 13, with the wedding just a week away, Ronnie needed to get a haircut and wanted to mow the lawn. This was earlier in the day of the helicopter ride. My friend Beth was going to come sit with me, but she had a bit of a cold and thus couldn't, so she called Cindy to see if she would be able to come, which she did.

Ronnie went to the barbershop at a time of day it was always open, but for some reason it was closed this particular day. He then went home to mow only to discover that some kind friend or neighbor (we still don't know who) had mowed the lawn for us. That left only his shower. It was just after he had finished and was getting dressed that the call came from Cindy that things had "headed south fast" and he needed to get to the hospital immediately.

If his plans had gone as he intended—if he had gotten the haircut and then been mowing—he would not have had his phone with him and would not have gotten the call, at least not until much later. At the very least, it would have been before he had a chance to take a shower. God is in the details, and He cares about even the small things.

At least three of the miracles were very practical in nature. The office where I work had just gotten big enough to have a group health plan. Prior to this, I had an individual plan that had pages of exclusions. The new plan was much better. It went into effect on April 1, and I was diagnosed April 10.

Second, our new health plan included a health savings account. Our office manager asked just a few days after my diagnosis if I had gone by the bank to set up my account. With so much going on, I hadn't done that yet. I went over to the bank at about 4:30 that afternoon. In the process of signing the paperwork, I was asked if I wanted to make a contribution for the previous year. This can be done up until

April 15, which happened to be that very day. HSA funds can only be spent on health-related expenses. I had the amount in my regular savings account and knew I would be spending all of it on the deductible anyway, so I made the contribution to the tax-free account with fifteen minutes to spare before the 5:00 deadline. We refiled our 2013 taxes and received an unexpected refund!

A third situation was also financial in nature and again more than a coincidence. Just a couple of weeks prior to leaving for Omaha, a coworker asked me a random question about whether HSA funds could be used for a certain type of expense. He recalled me using my HSA funds for my wig, and so he knew that I at least knew where to look.

I pulled up the website that listed eligible expenses, and while looking for the answer to his question, I happened to see on the list "meals and lodging expenses for medical travel." Because I would be considered outpatient at the transplant center in Omaha up until the actual chemo began, I realized we could use the HSA funds for our room and board expenses, which insurance didn't cover. The outpatient time ended up being two weeks prior to the chemo beginning, as well as a week after I was changed from inpatient to outpatient the last week we were up there.

As we were preparing for the long stay in Omaha, my only apprehension was that we would be far away from the friends and family that had been so present and supportive.

About that time, I heard from a friend I had known when I lived in Oklahoma almost thirty years earlier, Regina. She had just learned of my illness and sent a message via Facebook asking how I was doing. For some reason, after not having any contact with her for all those years, I shared that our next step was to spend a month in Omaha. I had to sit down when

I read her reply: "Cathy, I live in Omaha now!" As it turned out, the day we went up there was her birthday.

During one of the intake appointments in Omaha, we told the woman helping us that we would like to go to church while we could, because I would be considered outpatient until the start of the actual chemo. She told us the name of her church, and we looked it up online and decided to go there the following Sunday.

It was a large church. We got there late and slipped in one of the doors near the back. Whom should we see sitting right there but this woman with her family. Not only that, but when she introduced her family to us, included in the group were her in-laws, who were visiting from Bella Vista, Arkansas, just thirty minutes from where we live.

Shortly after this, Regina came to visit us at the transplant center. During the conversation, we mentioned that we had attended church and really enjoyed the service. She asked where we'd gone, and when I told her, her jaw dropped. It was the same church she attended; she had simply been out of town the day we went.

While in Omaha, I got a message from a former pastor, Brother Gibbie, who said he had a longtime friend who was now serving at a church in Omaha. He asked if it would be okay to ask his friend Byron to visit us. We said of course. As it turned out, of all the churches in Omaha, Byron was the music minister at the same church we had visited and that Regina and her husband Joe attended! In fact, Regina played the piano for the choir, and so she and Byron knew each other well.

When Byron came to visit, he looked and sounded so much like Brother Gibbie that I couldn't believe it. It was so comforting, like talking to someone I had known for a long time. Besides that, he told us to let him know of anything we needed, and someone in the church would see to the need. I remember him mentioning specifically that even if it were a car, they would make one available to us.

God had provided even the church family we knew we would miss so much. His hand was obvious in all of this; these were *not* coincidences!

CHAPTER 15

And the (Heart)Beat Goes On

In October 2018 I celebrated my fourth "birthday" since the cancer year. It is not lost on me that these are bonus years for me. One does not step back from having stood so very close to death's door without being changed. Life goes on. I don't procrastinate like I used to either, so a lot has happened in these four years!

I mentioned early in my story that my mom had been having some health issues. She and I had kept in touch through the year, often comparing hospital stays and medical procedures. One of the things I took to Omaha with me was a birthday card to send her, because her birthday was just days after we left to go up for the transplant.

We arrived home from Omaha on October 29. I went back to work on November 10. Ten days later, I received a call at work on a Thursday afternoon that Mom had been taken to the emergency room again but this time she had decided against any further treatment. She was being admitted to hospice.

After rushing home to hurriedly pack a bag, Ronnie and I left for Oklahoma City. We stayed in the room with Mom three nights and were there along with other family members when she breathed her last and graduated to heaven on Sunday, November 23. It was just twenty-five days after we returned home from Omaha.

My brother and I were adopted, but no one would ever have known it talking to Mom. She started out as our stepmother when I was ten and then adopted us after our dad died, when I was twenty.

She had been too ill to make the trip to attend Derick and Jill's wedding, and so by the time I took them over to Oklahoma City for Jill to meet her, it was after they'd announced they were expecting. It was August 2014, not long before I was to leave for Omaha, and at the time Jill had terrible morning sickness. Mom wondered aloud if she could be carrying twins. I suggested it was a possibility because twins ran in Jill's family. After giving it some thought, Mom said, "I don't think we have any twins in our family."

I was truly her daughter. I like to think she chose to stick around until she made sure I was going to make it. That's the kind of mom she was. Now you know why this book is dedicated to her.

The best thing of all happened in January 2015. Ronnie and I were in Omaha for my hundred-day follow-up visit after the stem cell transplant. The appointment was on a Monday, but we had driven up on Saturday to have dinner with our friends Joe and Regina and go to church with them on Sunday.

Early Sunday morning, I got a text from my son Dan. He had sent it to Derick, Jill, and me, asking us to pray for him. I was seven hours away. You can imagine the thoughts that went through this mom's head when I got that text!

I texted back, saying, "I pray for you every day. What's up?" No answer. I checked my phone all through church, but still nothing. I texted him following the service, asking if he was okay. He replied he was "more than okay" and would call later. Again my mind raced with possibilities.

We went out to lunch after church and headed back to the transplant center with still no call from him. (I had forgotten that he was interviewing candidates for his camp staff that day.) Finally, at about 4:00 in the afternoon, I got another text asking if it was a good time to call. I replied, "Yes!" He called right away and asked if I was sitting down. I almost shouted, "Would you *please* tell me what is going on?"

"Mom, I got saved today!"

I could have jumped up and down, and for all I remember I may have. As I recall, he described how he had been running from God, and he had finally quit running and surrendered, letting Jesus come in and take over. He went on to talk about it for forty-five minutes—and he has never been one to talk much!

Dan had done what a lot of people have done and prayed a prayer when he was a child, saying that he believed Jesus was the Son of God, died on a cross, and rose from the grave. He now realized that had been a decision of his head and not his heart. He had grown up in church and knew all the right things to do and say, but in his words, he had "been living a double life." He had never turned his life over to Jesus.

As his mom, I had felt for some time that this might be the case. I had even asked him if he was sure he was saved, and he had told me he was. But still there was that uncertainty in my mind and heart. So I prayed and prayed and prayed. For years I prayed.

And on January 25, 2015, those prayers were answered! There was no doubt it was the real thing this time, and Dan immediately started calling people to apologize and tell them how they could have the same peace he now had. As he posted online a year later, "I was on a path to self-destruction, but the King of the world had different plans. You can chase after anything you want in this life and even get what you're after, but you will never find contentment or true peace until you come to the cross, broken."

He called me the next day and talked again for another forty-five minutes as we were driving home from Omaha. It was obvious he had been carrying a heavy burden for a long time, and that burden had now been lifted.

It was lifted from this mother's heart as well. I was so happy God had let me live to see this!

Dan often stopped by my office when he was in town. This was summer of 2015, about six months after he was saved. We both have reason to smile!

The next big event was the birth of Israel David Dillard, my first grandchild. He was due at the end of March but finally arrived on April 6, 2015, which was the day after Easter that year. I was thrilled to be in the delivery room when he first entered the world.

Later that fall, I was still seeing Dr. Travis every twelve weeks and continuing to gain weight and strength. When Derick and Jill moved to Central America for a year to do mission work, I asked the doctor if there was any problem with me traveling outside the country. If they were going to take my only grandchild to another country, I was going to go check out the situation! I traveled down with them in October 2015 and helped with the baby as they settled in.

When they moved from Guatemala to El Salvador, I made another trip down to look things over and to be with them on Israel's first birthday in April 2016. They had been down there six months by this time, and so Christmas had been a long-distance holiday via phone and video chat!

Meanwhile, things were moving along for Dan as well. In November 2015, on our way to celebrate Thanksgiving with family in Oklahoma City, Dan shared with Ronnie and me that he had met a girl named Deena. Fast-forward to May 2016, when Dan took me to lunch to tell me he planned to propose to Deena. I had met her by this time and was thrilled.

He bought the ring but then had to spend all of June away at camp because it was part of his job with the Boy Scouts. He was worried I would let his secret slip when I took Deena with me to a family wedding in Oklahoma. Deena did wonder why I insisted she be in the family photos!

On July 12, he proposed, and she said yes. The wedding date was set for November 12, four months later. Because I had missed out on almost all of Derick and Jill's wedding festivities, I told Deena up front that I wanted to be as involved as she would let me.

To her credit (or as we say in the South, bless her heart), she let me in on everything! Her mom and I hosted the engagement party together. I got to go along on dress shopping and cake tasting, and I went to three showers.

I thoroughly enjoyed planning and decorating for the rehearsal dinner, which I actually got to attend this time! I cannot describe the pure joy of walking down the aisle on my son Dan's arm. Neither did I take for granted being able to stand for the photos afterward.

Dan and Deena's wedding, November 12, 2016. I don't think they were aware of anyone else in the room!

At one of my appointments with Dr. Travis, I had asked him if there was a milestone toward which I should be looking. He told me two years after the stem cell transplant, the likelihood of recurrence significantly dropped. I knew the chance of relapse dropped from 70 percent to 30 percent with the transplant, and the two-year mark meant it went to something less than that.

And so it was that in the middle of the four months of wedding festivities and preparations, we quietly celebrated my two-year mark on Sunday, October 9, 2016. I marked the occasion by having Derick, Jill, and Israel over for lunch. Imagine their surprise when I put on the dress I had worn for their wedding! We took a picture with me standing up this time and twenty-five pounds heavier than the last time I'd had on the dress.

Derick and Jill with me, marking two years since the
stem cell transplant. I am wearing the dress I wore to their
wedding, except I am twenty-five pounds heavier here!

At the end of October 2016, just two weeks before Dan and Deena's wedding, Derick and Jill once again called me with news that a baby was on the way, and was due to arrive the following summer. Samuel Scott Dillard was born Saturday, July 8, 2017. I was so happy to not only be here to meet him but to have the strength and stamina to keep two-year-old Israel while his mom and dad were at the hospital and during the time afterward when they were getting settled in at home with a new baby.

Sam had just turned six months old in January 2018 when Dan called one day to say he was in town and asked if I was available for lunch. It was not unusual for him to do this; we had done it several more times since the lunch where he told me he was going to propose to Deena, so I didn't think much of it.

Deena was with him this time, and they said they had a gift for me. I still didn't suspect anything because my birthday had been a couple of weeks earlier. Neither did I notice Deena holding her phone where she could video me as I opened the package.

It was a charm that said "Grandmother." I said something about how much I liked it and couldn't wait to add it to my bracelet. It was at this point that they said something. I don't recall what exactly they said because that was the moment I realized what they were trying to tell me: they were going to have a baby!

Once again, I treasured every moment of anticipation during Deena's pregnancy, and I was thrilled when she asked me to be with her during labor and delivery along with Dan and her mother and sister.

On September 5, 2018, I was there to witness the miracle of birth at the moment my grandson Jaxon Michael Dillard took his first breath.

I like to say "These seven are my heaven." Five of these
seven have come into my family since the cancer.

There have been so many other precious moments in the last few years. Even the simplest things are precious now, and I will be ever aware of how close I came to missing out on all of them.

On a more practical note, I had always thought I pretty much had my affairs in order. Having been widowed, I had thought I had all the details of life organized for the most part. But after nearly making my own exit from this world, I realized I would not have been leaving things nearly as neatly as I want to.

I am still working on that, and I try now to encourage others to get things in order in every sense of the word, because you just never know!

CHAPTER 16
You Just Never Know—But You Can!

I don't know why I got cancer. Doctors tell me non-Hodgkin's lymphoma is not hereditary, and they can't point to anything that causes it. Neither do I know why God chooses to heal some people and not others. I do know that God is God, and He created us and can do as He wills. I know that He healed me, and I find myself telling the story over and over again of how He did it.

I have experienced what I now know to be survivor's guilt when others with illnesses like mine or even less severe have not survived. As mentioned earlier, when sharing my story with other cancer patients or their families, I never suggest that their outcome will be the same. I do tell them that God is the same as He was throughout the Bible, and He never changes. Therefore why would we think He couldn't or wouldn't still do miracles?

None of us know when our time will come. It is important to be ready for the inevitable reality of death. More than having your financial and personal affairs in order, it is crucial to have your eternity settled. Just as the miracles I shared were not coincidences, the fact that you are reading this book at this time in your life is not a coincidence either.

In an earlier chapter, I shared the peace I had when I heard the news over the phone that I had cancer. This was the same peace I had when I learned the cancer was stage four, and when one doctor told me that it wouldn't do any good to consult an oncologist. I cannot tell my story without sharing the source of that peace—and how you can have it too.

I grew up in a family who went to church. I had heard almost since I was born that God loved me. I also had learned many Bible verses that explained that everyone is a sinner. I am embarrassed to admit I actually remember trying to think of any sins I might have committed and could not come up with any. Keep in mind that I was about seven or eight years old!

Then one Sunday when I was eight and a half years old, I was sitting in church like so many Sundays before. I don't remember what the sermon was about or what songs had been sung. I simply remember becoming suddenly and starkly aware that my sin stood between me and the God whom I loved and whom I knew loved me.

I told my parents as soon as we got into the car. After lunch, with my toddler brother down for a nap, they sat down with me to talk. They soon realized I had come to understand in a very real and personal way that this was the reason Jesus died: to remove the sin barrier that stood between God and me.

I prayed then and there, in 1965 on our white Naugahyde couch, to ask Jesus to forgive my sins and become Lord of my life.

I knew something special had happened when, at school the following day, I felt so different that I thought it must surely show! A burden had been lifted off my eight-year-old heart. I kept looking around to see if any of my third-grade classmates had noticed, but it was apparently not as obvious on the outside as it was to me on the inside.

God has been faithful to me in so many ways these fifty-plus years since. I can't tell you how many times people have told me I am a strong woman, but it is God who is the source of that strength. He is the source of the peace I had throughout the entire cancer year.

You can have that same peace, and you can have it now. You don't have to talk to anyone, you don't have to wait till you're in church, and you don't have to pray a special prayer or say special words.

If God has made you aware, like He did for Dan and me, that your sin separates you from Him, then tell Him that and repent of your sin. Be truly sorry that you have sinned against Him. Stop running. Tell Him you believe in your heart—not just in your head—that Jesus took the punishment for your sin while He hung on the cross, and that He rose from the dead. Jesus is alive today, will come into your life by His Holy Spirit, and lead you if you truly want to follow Him.

Although this is something you can do on your own, when it's the real thing, you will want to tell someone. Find a Bible-teaching church if you're not attending one already, let the pastor know, and get connected there. It will help you grow if you spend time every day reading the Bible and talking to God in prayer too.

This is the beginning of a journey of becoming more like Jesus every day. I am blessed and humbled to say that after more than fifty years, I am still on that journey!

When I was little, I loved to invite people to church. Now I invite them to heaven!

EPILOGUE

On that Easter Sunday in 2014, when I told my church about the cancer, I shared that I had told God I was ready to go to heaven, but there were some people I was praying to see saved. Dan was one of those. I praise God that he is off my list now!

I still have the list. In fact I have added to it. Some of you holding this book in your hands are on that list. Know that I am still praying for you.

I have a favor to ask. If the Holy Spirit uses this book to make you aware that you don't have the same peace I had through my cancer year, call me. We'll have coffee and talk.

And, God willing, we will cross your name off my list together!